Using Peer Mediation in
Classrooms and Schools

Using Peer Mediation in
Classrooms and Schools

Strategies for Teachers, Counselors, and Adminstrators

James Gilhooley ▪ Nannette S. Scheuch

CORWIN PRESS, INC.
A Sage Publications Company
Thousand Oaks, California

For information:

Corwin Press, Inc.
A Sage Publications Company
2455 Teller Road
Thousand Oaks, California 91320
E-mail: order@corwinpress.com

Sage Publications Ltd.
6 Bonhill Street
London EC2A 4PU
United Kingdom

Sage Publications India Pvt. Ltd.
M-32 Market
Greater Kailash I
New Delhi 110 048 India

Printed in the United States of America

Library of Congress Cataloging-in-Publication Data

Gilhooley, James.
   Using peer mediation in classrooms and schools: Strategies for teachers, counselors, and administrators / by James Gilhooley and Nannette S. Scheuch.
      p.   cm.
Includes index.
   ISBN 0-7619-7650-7 (cloth: alk. paper)
   ISBN 0-7619-7651-5 (pbk.: alk. paper)
   1. Peer counseling of students.   2. Mediation.   3. Conflict management—Study and teaching.   I. Scheuch, Nannette S.   II. Title.
   LB1027.5.G48   2000
   371.4'047—dc21   99-050551

This book is printed on acid-free paper.

00   01   02   03   04   05   10   9   8   7   6   5   4   3   2   1

Corwin Editorial Assistant: Julia Parnell
Production Editor: Denise Santoyo
Editorial Assistant: Cindy Bear
Typesetter/Designer: Janelle LeMaster
Cover Designer: Tracy E. Miller
Indexer: Teri Greenberg

Contents

PART 2: How Teachers, Counselors, and Administrators
Can Implement and Evaluate Their Mediation Programs

Preface

All students are entitled to a safe learning environment. Unfortunately, not all children have one. Many children across the United States are frightened to come to school because they are subjected to many forms of violence, such as bullying, teasing, and other senseless unkind acts. Adults cannot solve all problems that students face. We must empower them with the ability to solve their own problems. Peer mediation provides skills that enable students to resolve conflict without the use of weapons. Although such precautions as police presence in schools, identification badges, sign-in sheets, and metal detectors all may enhance school security, we believe that such methods treat the symptoms but neglect the causes of violence. Peer mediation addresses the causes by offering a process that focuses on prevention. By promoting student ownership, peer mediation diffuses conflict before it can escalate into violence.

■ *PURPOSE*

This book is unique in that it not only offers a hands-on training agenda with training posters that can be adapted to elementary or secondary grades, but it gives a step-by-step approach to introducing peer mediation to administrators, faculty and staff, students, parents, and the community. It supplies information on how to implement the process at all grade levels and how to evaluate an existing program, and makes suggestions for expanding the use of mediation within the school and community.

Our major hurdle after we had been trained in peer mediation was being faced with implementing the program. We had no idea where to begin because it was not addressed in our original training. After years of experience training schools in peer mediation and being asked how to implement the new process, we decided that a book that covers both training for and the implementation of peer mediation would be a valuable tool.

■ WHO SHOULD READ THIS BOOK AND WHY

Using Peer Mediation in Classrooms and Schools: Strategies for Teachers, Counselors, and Administrators appeals to those individuals who want to develop or implement a peer mediation program. Whether at the elementary or secondary level, administrators, teachers, student teachers, counselors, curriculum development personnel, parents, and students will find this book to be both informative and easy to use. The appeal of the book comes from its usefulness, readability, adaptability, sequence and design, ready-made forms, classroom readiness, and user friendliness for both adults and students. This book provides comprehensive guidelines and forms for everything that is needed for a peer mediation program: to initiate it, market it, train individuals, implement the program, evaluate it, and expand an existing program. Few, if any, books are as comprehensive as this one.

■ DESCRIPTION OF THE CONTENT

The book is divided into two parts. Part 1 addresses how teachers, counselors, and administrators can develop their own peer mediation programs, and Part 2 focuses on the implementation and evaluation of peer mediation. The Resource contains training posters that can be reproduced or enlarged.

Part 1

Chapter 1, "Overview and History," describes peer mediation, the mediation process, and why mediation is so successful. A rationale is discussed as well as the impact of empowering students to solve their own problems without adult intervention. A brief history of our program and a chronological diary are given as means of informing readers of the time frame for implementing a peer mediation program.

PART 1

What Peer Mediation Is and
How Teachers, Counselors,
and Administrators Can
Develop Their Programs

OVERVIEW AND HISTORY

■ *PEER MEDIATION IN HANDLING CONFLICT*

Conflict is a normal and unavoidable part of our daily lives, and we all have choices as to how we deal with it. However, most students tend to limit their options to one of two. They either avoid a confrontation entirely or dive into the conflict headfirst, dealing with it aggressively or physically.

In peer mediation, students are each given a chance to tell their side of the story. Ground rules are established to level the playing field. When each disputant has told his or her side of the story, solutions are discussed and agreed on. Mediators are trained as facilitators of the process using active listening skills, paraphrasing, and eliciting feelings and solutions. When solutions are agreed on, a signed, written agreement is the end result. Peer mediation, which includes conflict resolution skills, offers students options where they can learn to value diversity and resolve differences peacefully. Although not a panacea, mediation is a valuable tool in combating racism and violence. Each disputant comes away from the experience a winner. Mediation has been proven a more effective strategy than detention, suspension, or expulsion and can cause an increase in instructional time by decreasing the frequency of classroom disruptions.

■ *RATIONALE OF MEDIATION*

For peer mediation to be successful within the school, it is imperative that administration, faculty, and staff have a clear understanding of the process and how it enhances academic performance and decreases disruptions. Mediation empowers students to solve their own disagreements without adult intervention. This is not to say that professionals ignore the social problems of their students but, rather, empower students to help themselves. When children and adolescents are not preoccupied with the angst created by conflict, they are more focused on learning. So it is important that the faculty and support staff of the school understand and support the rationale of mediation before the concept is introduced to the students.

■ *INITIATING OUR PROGRAM*

Peer mediation was started in the Scranton School District in the fall of 1993 in response to the growing number of arguments, fights, and name calling incidents that were disrupting the educational process. As violence reached epidemic proportions in our society, it became an increasing concern within our schools as well. South Scranton Intermediate School piloted the initial peer mediation program within the district. In September of 1993, Educational Mediation Services of Lancaster, Pennsylvania, trained the faculty and student body in the mediation process. By October, 24 students and six faculty members were chosen to complete a 3-day training session, and on October 28, 1993, the peer mediation program began. In the first year, nearly 100 mediations took place; 98% were mediated successfully to a signed agreement.

The initial training was funded through a state grant for drug-free schools, and in 1995, the district received a large enough grant through the State Department of Education's Safe Schools Initiative to train two high schools, three intermediate schools, and 13 elementary schools in peer mediation. During the 1996-1997 school year, Neil Armstrong Elementary School became the first elementary building in the district to implement the peer mediation process.

■ *A CHRONOLOGY OF NEIL ARMSTRONG ELEMENTARY SCHOOL'S MEDIATION PROGRAM*

- September: Introduced peer mediation to faculty in a meeting at the beginning of the school year. Encouraged staff to discuss mediation with students.

- October: Held student assembly to introduce mediation and showed an example of mediation via role playing. Sought volunteers to be trained as mediators.

- November: Trained mediators and began mediations.

■ QUALITIES OF AN EFFECTIVE MEDIATOR

Students need to understand the role of a mediator and its importance. Students can learn to be responsible individuals who are capable of solving their own problems without the help of adults. When encouraging students to volunteer for training as mediators, the following qualities of an effective mediator should be stressed:

An effective mediator is someone who feels good about himself or herself and likes to help others. This is a service role.

- An effective mediator is a person who cares about his or her school and wants to make it a more peaceful and orderly place.

- An effective mediator is a conscientious student who keeps up to date with her or his work. It is not a requirement to be an honor student.

- An effective mediator is a person who can work under strict rules of confidentiality.

- An effective mediator must be willing to participate in 3 days of training and attend occasional meetings with an adviser to strengthen his or her mediation skills.

■ ADMINISTRATIVE AND FACULTY ROLES

Administration and faculty must understand their roles in the mediation process for it to be successful. Because a large percentage of referrals will come directly from the principal's and vice principal's offices, the administration has to be supportive for the process to be effective. An administrator from each building should complete the training sessions so that the process is completely understood. In addition to the administrator, the more support and input given by the faculty, the more likely it is that the process will be a success. Students and adults are trained together. If the students get the feeling that the faculty has faith in the process, they will as well. Once the process has been established, its success will speak for itself.

■ *THE USE OF ROLE PLAYS*

A good way to demonstrate the mediation process to the students and faculty is through the use of a role play (see Exhibits 1.1 and 1.2) that portrays a typical school conflict acted out by members of the student body. The role plays can be acted out by members of the student body who have not actually been trained, or they can be acted out by experienced mediators from another school. In either case, time should be given for the students to practice their roles and feel comfortable in front of an audience. Students should be encouraged to refer to their scripts but to read them as little as possible. The specific words don't have the impact that the authenticity of expressed feelings in an actual situation will have.

To ensure an effective role play, the following three steps should be taken:

1. Choose participants who are comfortable performing in front of an audience

2. Give the participants a chance to review their scripts and practice their roles

3. Provide the students with whatever props are necessary for an effective presentation (table, chairs, microphone, etc.)

A question and answer period should follow to clarify how the process will fit into the school's schedule. Reviewing typically asked questions (see Chapter 6) will make the experienced mediators feel more self-assured in front of their audience.

Exhibit 2.1. Role Play for Secondary Level

Rachael and Lindsey enter from the right. They are arguing with each other.

Mediator 1:	Hi, Rachael. Hi, Lindsey. You've been referred to peer mediation by one of your friends who was concerned about your arguing. Rumor has it there may be a fight.
Lindsey:	(angrily) Yeah, she's mad at me, and it's not my fault.
Rachael:	Well, why shouldn't I be mad at you?
Mediator 2:	(speaks to the group) Why don't we sit down and talk about this? I'm (name), and this is (name). We are not going to tell you how to solve your problem, but we can help you solve your own problem if you are both willing to let us.
Mediator 1:	Has either of you been to peer mediation before?
Lindsey:	No.
Rachael:	No.
Mediator 2:	Let me explain how this works. Each of you will get a chance to tell your side of the story without interruption, and you will discuss solutions to your problem that each of you will be happy with.
Mediator 1:	Before we start, there are some ground rules that you both need to agree to. First, do you both agree to work hard to solve your problem?
Rachael:	Yes.
Lindsey:	Yes.
Mediator 1:	Also, there is no name calling or put-downs. Can you both agree to that?
Lindsey:	(sarcastically) I can, but I know Rachael won't go along with anything!
Rachael:	(angrily) OK, fine! If you can, I can!
Mediator 2:	You must both agree not to interrupt when the other person is speaking and be as honest as you can. Can you both agree?
Rachael:	Yeah.
Lindsey:	Me, too.
Mediator 1:	Everything said here is confidential. We won't discuss what is said here with anyone. Rachael, would you like to start by telling your side of the story?
Rachael:	OK. We have been best friends forever. Two weeks ago, I told her that I really thought Bill Claus was cute and I would really love to go out with him. The next thing I heard was that she went out with Bill over the weekend.

Lindsey:	I only went to Bill to help you!
Mediator 2:	Lindsey, you agreed not to interrupt. You will have your turn. Go ahead Rachael, finish your story.
Rachael:	Like I was saying, I'm furious with Lindsey. She says one thing and does another. I just can't trust her again.
Mediator 1:	So, you confided in Lindsey that you liked Bill and wanted to go out with him, and then you found out that he went out with her instead. How did that make you feel?
Rachael:	I'm hurt and angry. I thought she was my friend, but she's a real loser.
Mediator 2:	Rachael, you agreed to no name calling.
Rachael:	Well, I'm upset!
Mediator 2:	Lindsey, would you like to tell your side of the story?
Lindsey:	Yes, I would! What Rachael said is mostly true, but she doesn't know the whole story. Rachael did tell me that she wanted to go out with Bill. I know Bill pretty well and thought that I would talk to him to see if he wanted to go out with Rachael. I told her I was going to do that, and she agreed. Well, when I started talking to Bill, he started flirting with me, and before I had a chance to ask him about Rachael, he asked me out.
Mediator 2:	So, you really went to see Bill to help Rachael, but before you knew it, he was asking you out instead. Is that what you are saying?
Lindsey:	That's what happened.
Mediator 2:	How did it make you feel when Bill asked you out?
Lindsey:	Well, I was surprised and flattered. I've always thought Bill was cute, but I didn't expect this. I never wanted to hurt Rachael, and I thought if I explained to her what happened, she would understand. The only problem was that I never saw her to tell her. She was away with her family.
Mediator 1:	So you feel badly about how this might affect Rachael, but you really did want to date Bill?
Lindsey:	That's right.
Mediator 1:	Is there anything else that either of you would like to say about the situation?
Lindsey:	I just wish Rachael could understand my situation. I understand why she feels betrayed, but it wasn't part of the plan.
Mediator 2:	Rachael?
Rachael:	I don't have anything more to say.
Mediator 2:	Rachael, what would make this situation better for you?

Rachael:	Well, she could apologize for what she did, and she could stop dating Bill. We always go to the mall together on Friday night, and now who will I go with if she's out with Bill?
Lindsey:	Look, Rachael, I thought you realized by now that I am sorry for this mess. I officially apologize, but if Bill asks me out again, I want to be able to go without jeopardizing our friendship.
Mediator 1:	Lindsey, what would make the situation better for you?
Lindsey:	Well, for one thing, she called me a loser a few minutes ago, and second, she said she could never trust me again, and I've never given her a reason not to trust me. I think I deserve an apology.
Rachael:	I'm sorry about calling you a loser, and now that I've heard the whole story, I can see that you really were trying to help me. Can we still go to the mall on Friday nights together?
Lindsey:	Sure!
Rachael:	And if for some reason Bill should ask me out, then I could say "yes" without you getting upset with me?
Lindsey:	If it was OK for me to go, then it's OK for you to go, too!
Mediator 1:	So you both agree that Friday nights are for you to go to the mall together. Lindsey has apologized for the mix-up, and you both agree that it is fair for either of you to see Bill.
Mediator 2:	Do you both feel better about this situation?
Rachael & Lindsey:	Yeah.
Mediator 1:	Good job. You have worked hard to solve your problem.

Mediators shake hands with the disputants.

Exhibit 2.2. Role Play for Elementary Level

Students are on the playground playing kick ball, and Erica and Colin are arguing. Two mediators approach them and ask if they would like help solving their problem.

Mediator 1:	Would each of you like us to help you solve your problem?
Erica & Colin:	Sure!
Mediator 2:	You need to agree to some ground rules first. Can you agree to no name calling or put-downs?
Colin:	Well, I can if she can!
Erica:	I can agree to that!
Mediator 2:	Can you both agree to no interruptions?
Erica & Colin:	Yes.
Mediator 1:	Can you agree to tell the truth and work hard to solve the problem?
Erica:	Yes, I don't want Colin to stay mad at me.
Colin:	Sure.
Mediator 2:	Can you both agree to no swearing or violence?
Erica & Colin:	(as they nod their heads) Yeah, sure.
Mediator 1:	Erica, will you tell us what happened?
Erica:	Well, we were playing kick ball, and I was on first base when Colin got up to kick. He kicked the ball really hard right at my face, and I fell and ripped the new jeans my mom just bought. Colin started laughing at me!
Mediator 1:	So what you're saying is that while you were on first, Colin got up and kicked the ball at your face, and you fell and ripped your new jeans. Is that correct?
Erica:	That's what happened, all right. I was really mad when Colin laughed at me.
Mediator 2:	Colin, can you tell us what happened?
Colin:	Well, our team was losing by a run, so when I got up to kick the ball, I wanted to kick Erica home to score, but Sam was pitching spinners. He always does that! And when I kicked, the ball went straight at Erica. I didn't try to hit her with the ball. I was mad at Sam!
Mediator 2:	You're telling us that you wanted to kick Erica home, and because Sam was pitching spinners, the ball went straight at Erica instead. You felt bad about that, and you were mad at Sam. Is that right?

Colin:	That's what I said.
Mediator 1:	Is there anything else you'd like to tell us?
Erica:	Yes. I was embarrassed because everyone was laughing at me—even Colin! I thought we were friends, but I guess not!
Mediator 2:	Colin, what about you, do you have any more you'd like to say?
Colin:	Yes, I do. I was not laughing at Erica. But it seemed as if everyone was. I felt bad for her.
Mediator 1:	OK, think about how you can solve this problem. Colin, can you think of some solutions?
Colin:	Well, I want to still be friends with Erica. I don't want her to be mad at me, and I want her to know that I was not laughing at her.
Mediator 2:	Erica, what about you? What are some solutions?
Erica:	I want to apologize to Colin for saying he laughed at me. I was embarrassed and blamed him for what happened. I would also like Colin to come with me and talk to Sam. He needs to stop pitching those spinners!
Mediator 2:	OK, Erica and Colin, can you both agree that you want to stay friends?
Erica & Colin:	Yes.
Mediator 1:	Erica, would you like to apologize to Colin now?
Erica:	Sure. I'm sorry, Colin.
Colin:	That's OK.
Mediator 2:	Colin, will you go with Erica to talk to Sam about pitching spinners?
Colin:	Let's talk to him as soon as we're finished here!
Erica:	Good idea!
Mediator 1:	Congratulations! You have solved your problem.

Mediators shake hands with the disputants as they all leave the area.

PART 2

How Teachers, Counselors, and Administrators Can Implement and Evaluate Their Mediation Programs

---

STEP TWO
Selecting and Training Mediators

■ *THE APPLICATION PROCESS*

Immediately following the demonstration of the mediation process to the students, have application forms (see Exhibit 3.1) available for students who might be interested. Students should be told how selections will be made. Once applications are turned in, review all applications for content. A core group of faculty, counselors, and staff who know the students well are best suited to make the selection of those to be trained as mediators. Once the number of applicants has been narrowed down based on the responses on the applications, an interview process works well in further narrowing down the field of prospective candidates. This is especially helpful at the secondary level. In the interview, candidates can be asked about their motives for applying and their feelings about becoming trained as mediators. It is very important that students chosen to be mediators are both respectful of others and respected by their peers.

Because attendance at all sessions is imperative to obtaining the skills needed to successfully mediate, it is important to inform students and staff of the training dates during the inservice presentation. Also, students should be informed as to where and when applications should be returned.

■ *COMMUNITY AND PARENTAL SUPPORT*

Informing parents of the peer mediation process is a crucial step in implementation. A letter explaining the process (see Exhibit 3.2) and a permission slip (see Exhibit 3.3) is sent home with all students who are interested in applying to become mediators. In addition, an article should

appear in the school newsletter or local newspaper (see Exhibit 3.4) to explain the process and inform the community that the school district will be implementing a peer mediation program in the near future. Community support can be very valuable, especially when it comes to funding.

Exhibit 3.1. Peer Mediator Application Form

Complete and return to the guidance office by _____.

Name _____

Grade _____   Homeroom _____

1. Are you willing to participate in 3 days of mediation training
   on the following dates?   _____   yes   no

2. Are you willing to make up all work that might be missed as
   a result of training and mediating?   yes   no

3. What other extracurricular activities are you currently involved in?

   _____

   _____

   _____

4. Write a paragraph explaining why being a peer mediator appeals to you and what
   qualities you possess that would make you a good mediator.

   _____

   _____

   _____

   _____

   _____

   _____

Gilhooley, J., & Scheuch, N. *Using Peer Mediation in Classrooms and Schools: Strategies for Teachers, Counselors, and Administrators.* © 2000 Corwin Press, Inc.

Exhibit 3.2. Letter to Parents

Dear Parent:

Your child has expressed an interest in being trained as a peer mediator. Peer mediation is a violence prevention program that enhances school climate and can increase academic performance as a result of a more relaxed atmosphere. Peer mediators are a diverse cadre of students selected to receive specialized training in conflict management. Using a problem-solving approach intended to clarify the nature of disputes, peer mediators do not solve problems for other students but help them to think of ways to solve problems for themselves in a peaceful manner. The emphasis is on listening and trying to understand the other person's perspective. Agreeing to use the peer mediation process is voluntary.

Peer mediators are not police officers or judges but rather facilitators of a unique process that helps students solve their own problems without adult intervention. Also, peer mediators gain personal insight and skills that enhance their own self-esteem and academic performance. Schools across the country with similar programs report significant decreases in suspensions and expulsions, reduced tensions, and improved school climate overall. In addition to making the school a safer place in which to learn, the skills gained in training can be applied throughout a student's personal life, making the community a safer place in which to live.

A permission slip is enclosed.

Gilhooley, J., & Scheuch, N. *Using Peer Mediation in Classrooms and Schools: Strategies for Teachers, Counselors, and Administrators.* © 2000 Corwin Press, Inc.

Exhibit 3.3. Parental Permission Form

I give permission for my child, _____, to participate in

the peer mediation training that will take place on _____.

I understand that all work missed as a result of the training must be made up.

Yes   No

Please return this form to _____

by _____.

If you have any questions, please feel free to contact _____

at _____.

Student's Name _____

Parent's Signature _____

Exhibit 3.4. Press Release

The _____ School District will be implementing a peer mediation program in the coming weeks. Peer mediation is a violence prevention program that enhances school climate and can increase academic performance as a result of a more relaxed school atmosphere. Peer mediators are a diverse cadre of special students trained in conflict management. Using a problem-solving approach intended to clarify the nature of disputes, peer mediators do not solve problems for other students but help them to think of ways to solve problems for themselves in a peaceful manner. The emphasis is on listening and trying to understand the other person's point of view. Using the peer mediation process is voluntary.

Peer mediators are facilitators of a unique process that helps students solve their own problems without adult intervention. Schools across the country with similar programs report significant decreases in suspensions and expulsions, reduced tensions, and improved school climate. In addition to making the school a safer place for students, it can contribute to a more peaceful community as skills learned in the process are applied throughout life.

The training will take place on _____ and will be provided by _____. Twenty-four students and six adults will be trained in the mediation process, which includes activities in active listening, conflict resolution, paraphrasing, and managing anger.

STEP THREE
Getting Started

■ *SAMPLE TRAINING AGENDA*

The following sample training agenda shows suggested topics covered and time required. It can be changed to meet your school's particular needs and the needs of the participants at both the elementary and secondary levels. The training posters referred to can be found in the Resource section.

Day 1

Session 1: 2 hours

Present the agenda for the 3 days of training (Training Poster 1) so participants know what to expect.

Present the ground rules (Training Poster 2). To create a safe and comfortable environment,

- Everyone should participate
- Students must respect the feelings and ideas of others
- Students should be supportive of others
- Confidentiality must be respected

Students should have fun!

Ask the group members if they would like any other ground rules added to make sessions comfortable for them.

Understanding Conflict

- To explore the nature of conflict
- To explore how students view and react to conflict
- To introduce conflict resolution styles

Activity 1

Ask participants to each draw a picture of how they view conflict. Divide the group into pairs. Ask the participants to explain their pictures to their partners and introduce themselves. Partners will then come to the front of the room and introduce their partner to the group, followed by an explanation of their pictures of conflict.

Activity 2 (Training Poster 3)

Ask the group what words come to mind when they hear the word *conflict*. These responses should be recorded and discussed to determine what kinds of words are mentioned most often.

Are they negative or positive?

Are they good or bad?

Explain that conflict is neither good nor bad. It's how conflict is dealt with that can be negative or positive.

Activity 3 (Training Poster 4)

1. Discuss three styles of conflict resolution with the group and give several examples of each:

   Avoidance

   Aggression

   Problem solving

2. At the secondary level, ask participants to pick different partners and assign each pair a style of conflict resolution. Each pair should then think of an example of that style and act it out in front of the large group.

   At the elementary level, ask the large group to think of examples or stories depicting examples of each style.

Session 2: 1 hour

Finding Solutions

- To begin thinking about problem solving

Activity 4 (Training Poster 5)

1. Describe to the group a conflict between two people (use age-appropriate examples). Have the group think of some possible solutions. The solutions will fall into one of the following categories:

    Win-lose—one person wins, the other loses

    Lose-lose—both parties lose

    Win-win—both parties win

Discuss each solution and why it falls into its category, and record responses.

2. For secondary students, ask groups of four to think of a conflict that they have experienced and to develop three solutions. Ask for volunteers to share their conflicts and solutions with the large group. Encourage discussion.

Mediation

-   To understand why mediation works

Activity 5 (Training Poster 6)

Discuss the following points:

-   Mediation examines the other's point of view.
-   Mediation results in a win/win outcome.
-   Mediation is voluntary.
-   Mediation stresses cooperation.
-   Mediation allows the exploring of options.
-   Mediation encourages participants to express emotions.
-   Mediation is based on respect.

Session 3: 2 hours

Dealing With Feelings

-   To understand that people have many feelings and to recognize those feelings
-   To distinguish between a thought and a feeling

Activity 6 (Training Posters 7 & 8)

1. The group must understand that feelings are a part of every conflict and that expressing feelings is crucial to resolving the problem. Explain that many times, disputants want to talk about what happened rather than how they felt. Next, ask the group to think of as many feelings as possible that arise when they experience conflict. Record their responses. Second, ask for feelings that are present when they are not in conflict, and record these emotions also. Discuss the wide range of human emotion.

2. For secondary training, ask the class to decide if a statement describes a thought or a feeling. Give many examples of both. If the example is a thought, try to have the class express the feeling behind the thought.

Example: *"I feel sad"* expresses a feeling. *"I feel like punching him"* expresses a thought; the feeling expressed here might be anger.

Mediators should say, "That's what you feel like doing, but how does this make you feel?"

Active Listening

- To understand listening
- To understand and contrast good and poor listening
- To be aware of nonverbal communication

Activity 7 (Training Poster 9)

Ask a member of the group to tell you a story about something that happened to him or her or about a concern. Warn the person privately that you will be displaying poor listening skills.

Example: Look around the room, interrupt, fidget, and so on.

Discuss what happened, including how the storyteller felt. Next, have the same person tell you the same story. This time, demonstrate good listening skills.

Example: Face the person, make eye contact, nod, use good body language, use facial expressions, sit still, and so on.

Now, discuss the differences, and include how the storyteller felt.

Activity 8

This activity works well at both elementary and secondary levels. Put the group into pairs and have them take turns talking to their partners about a good book that they have read or about a favorite movie. Have the listeners practice good active listening skills. Let them evaluate each other and then change partners until the skill is mastered.

Paraphrasing

- To understand the importance of paraphrasing in the mediation process
- To combine facts and feelings in the form of a paraphrase

Activity 9 (Training Poster 10)

1. Explain that paraphrasing is one of the most important skills a mediator can possess. It is the ability to state in one's own words what another person has said. It lets the speaker know that the mediator is listening. This skill allows the mediator to neutralize any inflammatory language.

2. Demonstrate paraphrasing to the group. Have a volunteer tell you a story, then paraphrase. You'll need to listen for the facts and the feelings. The mediator can say, "So you're feeling _____ because _____."

Pair participants and have them spread out for this activity. They will take turns talking about what makes them angry and paraphrasing what they hear. Continue with this activity until all have had a chance to be both speaker and listener, and everyone is able to paraphrase effectively.

Day 2

Agenda

1. Continue training exercises

Session 1: 1 hour

Points of View

- To help see others' perspectives
- To understand different sides of the story in a conflict

Activity 1

Explain that many conflicts are the result of different points of view. Two people can look at the same situation and see it completely differently. The role of the mediator is not to determine who is right or wrong but to help each disputant understand the other's perspective. Ask students to think of a dispute that was the result of not understanding the other person's point of view. Ask for a volunteer to share this experience with the group. Discuss focusing on points of view and that mediators accomplish this through having disputants paraphrase each other.

Session 2: 1 hour

Mediation Process—Introduction

- To observe the introductory stage
- To practice the introduction

Activity 2 (Training Posters 11 & 12)

1. Demonstrate the first stage in the mediation process. Ask two volunteers to be disputants. Introduce yourself to the disputants by saying,

Example: *"Hello, my name is _____. I'm a mediator. Do you want help solving your problem?"*

If both agree, explain that there are ground rules that both must agree to follow:

"Do you agree to no interruptions?"

"Do you agree to no name calling?"

"Do you agree to tell the truth?"

"Do you agree to work hard to solve the problem?"

Be sure to get an agreement from each disputant for each ground rule before continuing to the next rule.

2. Allow students to role-play the introductions. Divide the class into groups of four with an adult assigned to each group. The adult will facilitate the activity and offer suggestions and feedback.

The pair playing the mediators should decide before they begin how they will share the introduction. Each person should have the opportunity to play both a mediator and a disputant.

Session 3: 1 hour

Managing Anger

- To understand anger
- To become aware of positive ways to deal with anger

Activity 3 (Training Posters 13 & 14)

Explain that the group will take a look at what makes people angry and what is done with that anger. Ask students to write down all the things that make them angry. Give each student the opportunity to share what they have written. Record their responses. Discuss comments and acknowledge that they have the right to feel angry. It is what people do with their anger that is damaging. Next, ask the group to record what they do when they are angry. Now, discuss responses, asking which are positive ways of dealing with anger and which are negative. It is important that students realize that their response to anger does not have to be negative.

Activity 4

Have secondary students take the time to write out their own personal prescription for anger by writing down five positive responses to anger that would work for them. Encourage them to use these in the future when faced with anger, rather than reacting immediately without thinking the situation through. (Positive responses are ones that don't carry negative consequences and won't hurt anyone.)

"I" Messages

- To understand "I" messages
- To practice "I" messages

Activity 5 (Training Poster 15)

1. Explain that conflict is often made worse if inflammatory language is used. The common "you" message is an example:

Example: *"You are such a jerk, you're always late, and I'm sick of it!"*

This type of statement is sure to make matters worse!

The "I" message is more likely to make one's feelings known without making the other person angry:

Example: *"I feel angry when you're late and would appreciate it if you would be on time."*

Discuss the differences between the two statements. Stress that "I" messages are an important part of the mediation process even though they may seem difficult and need to be practiced.

2. Ask the class to break into pairs. Present the following situation:

Example: In your group of friends, one person has become quite bossy, always telling everybody what to do and how to do it. You are really sick of it.

Pairs are to give each other "I" messages explaining how they feel and why. Ask for examples and discuss some of the feelings experienced.

Students can use the following formula:

Example: *"I feel _____ when you _____."*

3. Have secondary students think of a conflict that they are currently experiencing or think of someone with whom they are upset. Have them write down an "I" statement that they can use when they have the opportunity. Don't ask them to share these with the group.

Session 4: 2 hours

Mediation Process—Storytelling

- To understand the process of storytelling

- To practice storytelling

Activity 6 (Training Poster 16)

1. Demonstrate the storytelling stage to the group using the following format:

   Ask Disputant 1, "What happened?" Paraphrase the disputant.

   Ask Disputant 1, "How did you feel?" "Why?" Paraphrase the disputant.

   Ask Disputant 2, "What happened?" Paraphrase the disputant.

   Ask Disputant 2, "How did you feel?" "Why?" Paraphrase the disputant.

   Say to Disputant 1, "Tell me what you heard [Disputant 2] say."

   Say to Disputant 2, "Tell me what you heard [Disputant 1] say."

   Ask both, "Is there anything either of you would like to add?"

2. Break into groups of four with an adult assigned to each group. Two will act as the disputants and two will act as the mediators. Role-play the first two stages of the mediation process. Process the activity as a large group. (Students can make up a role-play.)

   Brainstorming

   • To practice brainstorming

Activity 7 (Training Poster 17)

1. Explain the concept of brainstorming and how it's used in mediating conflict: *Brainstorming* is working together to come up with as many options to solve a problem as possible. The disputants should arrive at possible solutions and refrain from discussing or criticizing any of the ideas. The mediator writes down all of the ideas. The mediator reads the ideas aloud, going through the list to see if there are options that are agreeable to both.

2. For elementary students, show the group a bookend or other strange object that they may not have seen very often. Go around the room and ask each participant to think of what the object might be used for. Encourage any and all responses, regardless of how silly they might seem. Write these down. Discuss how important brainstorming is to the mediation process.

3. For secondary students, break into pairs to brainstorm what they will serve at a weekend party (snacks, beverages, etc.). Ask the students not to talk during the brainstorming session but, rather, take turns writing down their responses. After brainstorming is complete, have them go over the list and draw either a smile, if they like the suggestion, or a frown if they do not. Then, have them look at the list to decide which are good choices for the party. Discuss how brainstorming contributes to the problem-solving process.

Mediation Process—Problem Solving

- To practice planning together

Activity 8 (Training Poster 18)

1. Ask two group members to role-play being disputants, choosing and describing a sample dispute. Demonstrate the problem-solving process using the following format:

   Ask both, "What could you do to solve this problem?"

   For each idea, ask both, "Can you agree to that?"

   Continue in this manner until they can agree and choose ideas that they like the best.

2. Break into groups of four and practice the first three stages of mediation. Have one group role-play for the larger group, and encourage discussion.

Day 3

Agenda

1. Complete training exercises
2. Have participants evaluate training on forms provided
3. Present certificates
4. Discuss implementation of the mediation program

Session 1: 20 minutes

Mediation Process—Agreement

- To observe how an agreement is reached
- To practice reaching an agreement
- To practice writing an agreement

Activity 1 (Training Poster 19)

Demonstrate the agreement process using the following format:

1. Restate the agreed-on solutions.

2. Ask both, "Is the problem solved?"

3. Ask both, "What would you do to keep the problem from happening again?"

4. Congratulate both disputants.

5. Fill out the agreement form, being specific (see Exhibits 4.1 & 4.2).

6. Mediators and disputants sign the agreement.

Exhibit 4.1. Agreement Form

Date: _____

Mediation between:

_____ and _____

Agreement:

_____

_____

_____

_____

_____

_____

Signed:

  Disputants: _____

                _____

  Mediators: _____

                _____

Exhibit 4.2. Sample Completed Agreement Form

Date: _____01-04-99_____

Mediation between:

_____Bill Smith_____ and _____Mary Jones_____

Agreement:

Bill agrees to pay Mary $4.50 on Friday, 10-4-01, to pay for the lost book.

Mary will go with Bill to see the librarian on Tuesday, 10-4-01, to explain to her what has happened.

Both Bill and Mary agree that they will not borrow a library book from each other in the future.

Both Bill and Mary apologized to each other during the mediation.

Signed:

Disputants: _____*Bill Smith*_____

_____*Mary Jones*_____

Mediators: _____*Patsy Gilluide*_____

_____*Jose Hernandes*_____

Session 2: 15 minutes

Confidentiality

- To understand the importance of confidentiality
- (For secondary level) To discuss issues of concern regarding confidentiality

Activity 2

1. Discuss with the trainees the importance of confidentiality in the success of the mediation process. Students will not trust mediators if they disclose any information concerning mediations that take place. Mediators should also encourage the disputants not to disclose information from the mediation and tell friends only that "the problem has been solved." Oftentimes, well-meaning friends can actually continue to fuel the fire if details of the mediation agreement are disclosed. Breaching the ground rule of confidentiality is a serious offense for a mediator. This responsibility must be taken seriously.

2. When training secondary school mediators, it's very important to discuss their concerns regarding confidentiality. This helps schools establish confidentiality rules to suit individual needs. For example, an important phrase to include in the confidentiality clause is, "We must report any threats of harm or abuse." Schools must decide what other information they feel must be disclosed, such as drug abuse or sexual abuse. The simpler the clause, the easier for the mediators. They do not want to be regarded as "snitches;" however, they have genuine concerns for their peers. One suggestion is for mediators to refer peers whom they feel have problems to a counselor or student assistance team.

Session 3: 1 hour

Role-Play Full Mediation

- To provide trainees with the opportunity to mediate all stages of the mediation process
- To answer questions concerning mediation

Activity 3

1. Have students break into groups and practice the entire mediation process, including writing and signing the agreement. Process in a large group, asking what went well and what they might do better next time.

2. Answer specific questions that participants have regarding the mediation process.

Session 4: 20 minutes (Training Poster 20)

Evaluation & Certificates

1. Distribute training evaluations to be filled out by all participants (see Exhibit 4.3)

2. Distribute certificates (see Resource)

Exhibit 4.3. Training Evaluation Form

1. On a scale of 1 to 5, how would you rate the training?
   (1 = *poor*, 5 = *excellent*)

   _____

2. What parts of the training did you like best?

   _____

   _____

   _____

3. What parts of the training did you like least?

   _____

   _____

   _____

4. What would you do to make the training better?

   _____

   _____

   _____

5. Was the training too long?   Yes   No

   Too short?   Yes   No

6. How do you feel about being a peer mediator?

   _____

   _____

   _____

Let's Go

Once the students and the faculty have been trained, it is time to go! A committee comprised of administrators, student mediators, and trained faculty members should convene to set up the process. This last section of the chapter will help with the logistical decisions needed for a successful program.

Identifying Newly Trained Mediators

Once the decision has been made as to who will coordinate the program, it is probably best to take time to introduce the newly trained mediators to the school population and make sure that everyone knows exactly what can be expected of mediation. Don't be too hasty to start mediations until adequate time has been taken to ensure that *everyone* understands the new process and who the new mediators are. Here are some suggestions:

- Send a letter to parents explaining the program, and prepare a press release that includes a picture of the new mediators.

- Prepare a centrally located bulletin board with photographs of the new mediators and explanations about when and how mediations can take place.

- Make banners to hang in hallways.

- Prepare a video clip to be played for the student body as part of daily announcements, introducing the mediators and explaining the new process.

- Have the new mediators visit classrooms to demonstrate mediation and answer questions from their peers.

- Include an article in the school handbook explaining the mediation process.

- Have the mediators help design a pamphlet, including pictures, an explanation of mediation, and how referrals can be made.

- Design T-shirts for mediators to wear on special occasions.

Where Will Mediations Take Place?

A space must be designated within the school that is suitable for mediations. In choosing a site, consider safety, comfort, and accessibility. Some schools have a designated mediation room, used exclusively for the purpose of mediation. This is a luxury that many schools cannot provide with existing crowded conditions. If this is the case in your school, a quiet corner in the building can suffice.

A mediation area at the secondary level should be located in an area away from wherever discipline problems are handled. It is best if the room affords students some privacy but is still within reach if an adult is needed. The room should contain the following items:

- A table with four chairs

- A filing cabinet in which to keep signed agreements and extra agreement forms (Exhibit 4.2)

- A mediation packet that contains a quick outline of the mediation process (see Exhibit 4.4)

At the elementary level, mediations can take place in the classroom, in the hall, in the lunchroom, or on the playground. Some schools also have a mediation room where mediations can take place. There may actually be times when more than one mediation is taking place at the same time.

Scheduling Mediations

Another important consideration is when mediations will take place. There are several ways in which this can be approached. Certainly, some mediations will take place on the spot, especially at the elementary level, and there may be cases at the secondary level when an emergency mediation needs to take place without going through the referral process. Some schools schedule certain days as mediation days. This may not be effective for problems that arise on a given day and don't get mediated until several days later. Another suggestion is to designate specific periods each day with assigned mediators for those periods. However, the assigned mediators may not be the most appropriate for specific cases and particular disputants. One suggestion to avoid this from occurring is to schedule a mediation for the following day, considering the nature of the conflict and the disputants involved. That way, care can be taken to select appropriate mediators.

One last suggestion is to assign mediators to be "on duty" on a particular day of the week. Students can report to the coordinator at the start of the day to be given their mediation assignments and excuses from class (see Exhibits 4.5 & 4.6). These days can be rotated so that students will not be missing the same scheduled classes on their assigned days.

How Will Referrals Be Made?

Referral forms must be accessible to administration, faculty, and all students within the building. Placing referral forms (see Exhibit 4.7) in every classroom, the guidance office, the library, and the main office contributes to the process being effectively used. Once a referral is made, there needs to be a designated drop-off spot. A referral box is ideal. The referral box also must be located in a spot accessible to everyone, including the coordinator, who will be checking the box and scheduling the mediations.

Mediation boxes can be simply made out of cardboard or wood. It works well to have a box with a top slit into which the referral forms can be placed anonymously and with a lid that opens easily to retrieve the referrals. A wall-mounted box located in a centralized area works very well.

Exhibit 4.4. Mediation Packet—Quick Outline

1. Introduction Stage
   a. Introduce mediators.
   b. Refer to disputants by name.
   c. Review the ground rules.

2. Storytelling Stage
   a. Disputant 1 tells story.
   b. Mediator paraphrases for fact and feeling.
   c. Disputant 2 tells story.
   d. Mediator paraphrases for fact and feeling.

3. Brainstorming
   a. Go back and forth having disputants come up with options.
   b. Don't have them agree or disagree *yet*.
   c. When options are exhausted, have the disputants decide what they can agree on.
   d. Make sure they both agree to something.
   e. Ask, "Does this take care of the problem for both of you?"

4. Agreement Writing
   a. One mediator tells the other what each disputant has agreed to.
   b. The agreement is written on the agreement form.
   c. Agreements are specific (who, when, where, how).
   d. Mediators and disputants sign the agreement.
   e. Mediators, congratulate the disputants.
   f. Congratulate yourselves!

5. Follow-Up
   a. Within the next 2 days, ask the disputants how things are going with the agreement.

Gilhooley, J., & Scheuch, N. *Using Peer Mediation in Classrooms and Schools: Strategies for Teachers, Counselors, and Administrators.* © 2000 Corwin Press, Inc.

Exhibit 4.5. Peer Mediation Notice

Please send the following student(s) to

Ms./Mr. _____

during homeroom today.

Thank You,
Ms./Mr. _____

Exhibit 4.6. Peer Mediation Excuse

Please excuse _____

to the mediation room during period _____, if at all possible.

Any work that is missed will be made up.

Thank You,

Ms./Mr. _____

Time returning: _____

Gilhooley, J., & Scheuch, N. *Using Peer Mediation in Classrooms and Schools: Strategies for Teachers, Counselors, and Administrators.* © 2000 Corwin Press, Inc.

Exhibit 4.7. Peer Mediation Referral Form

Date: _____

Names of people being referred:

_____   Homeroom: _____

_____   Homeroom: _____

Name of person making the referral (this is confidential):

_____   Homeroom: _____

Reason for referral (be brief):

_____

_____

_____

_____

Place in the peer mediation box or give to _____

To be filled by Ms./Mr. _____ :

Mediators Assigned:

_____

_____

Period:_____   Room: _____

_____

Period:_____   Room: _____

STEP FOUR
The Referral Process

Once a referral has been made, several steps must be taken.

1. The coordinator chooses appropriate mediators for a case. Some considerations should be the age and gender of the disputants and their personalities. It would probably not be wise, for example, to schedule a sixth-grade mediator with eighth-grade disputants. Also, the mediators should reflect the race and gender of the disputants so that everyone feels comfortable and the disputants don't get a sense of bias within the mediation.

In addition, it is important that the mediators be told who will be involved and given a general idea of the nature of the conflict. If either of the mediators feel uncomfortable with either a disputant or the nature of the conflict, he or she should be replaced with another mediator. The comfort of the mediators is of utmost importance and should be respected.

2. The disputants are informed that they have been referred for mediation. Referrals are anonymous for students and teachers, so it is never disclosed who has made the referral. However, the principal or vice principal does not necessarily remain anonymous when directly referring students for mediation.

3. The mediation process is explained, and a verbal agreement to mediation is received. If a disputant does not agree to mediation, it is important to find out why. Very often, the individual does not understand the process and is reluctant due to fear and uncertainty. However, once the

process is explained and understood and the disputant realizes that the process is facilitated by other students, a verbal agreement to mediation is usually reached. If, however, a disputant still refuses the mediation, that decision should be respected. A referral coming from the principal or vice principal that requires disciplinary action if mediation is refused must be returned to the individual making the referral.

4. The mediators and the disputants are assigned a period and a place for the mediation, and they are given excuses to present to their teachers (Exhibits 4.5 & 4.6).

5. Should the time for mediation be a conflict for any of the students or their teachers, it is rescheduled at the earliest possible time.

What is the main source of referrals?

Most referrals at the secondary level come from the principal and vice principal, although referrals can come from anyone. Guidance counselors, teachers, students, and even parents have requested mediation.

Is everything confidential?

No! If anything is disclosed that is considered to be a potential danger to anyone, or if any type of abuse is disclosed, it must be reported. Everything else is confidential. Disputants are encouraged to tell their friends that the problem has been solved without disclosing the details of the mediation.

Why is it necessary to have teachers trained?

For the process to function successfully within the school, not only should teachers be trained, but an administrator, parents, and staff should also be invited to be trained. When adults gain the knowledge and skills used in the process, they can use the process themselves and are more committed to the program.

How are mediators chosen?

Any student can apply to be trained. It is *very* important that a diverse population of the student body is chosen in order for the program to be successful. An application process is suggested, with an interview to follow. Care should be taken to include those students who are committed to making a difference within their school regardless of their gender, race, or academic achievement. All students should be up to date with their school work, however.

How will a mediation program help the professional staff? Isn't this just one more responsibility?

Students helping other students frees the teachers to teach and the administrators to perform their administrative duties. This program actually gives professionals more time to focus on education while the students are empowered to help one another.

■ QUESTIONS FREQUENTLY ASKED BY STUDENTS

What if one person wants to go to mediation and the other doesn't?

Mediation is voluntary. If one person does not want to go to mediation, the conflict cannot be mediated.

What if a mediator gets into a fight?

Mediators are trained to manage their anger in positive ways without resorting to violence. However, conflict is a natural part of everyone's life and mediators can certainly be referred to mediation. There is nothing wrong with being mediated. It indicates that individuals are mature enough to handle their conflicts constructively. Mediators are expected to be positive role models who are respected by their peers. If a mediator gets into a physical fight, it is suggested that he be suspended from mediating for a period of time, depending on the circumstances. Violence is not an acceptable conflict resolution style in most cases.

Is it hard to be a mediator?

Mediators are specially trained and always work with a partner. It is not difficult, and the more experience that a mediator gains, the easier it becomes. It is, however, challenging and rewarding work.

What if a fight breaks out during the mediation?

Remember that mediation is voluntary and the disputants are being mediated because they want to solve their problem. It is extremely unlikely that a fight would occur, but if it did, an adult is always nearby.

What if something comes up during mediation that the mediators can't handle?

Mediators are trained to consult with an adult if anything comes up during the mediation that they may be unsure of handling. All they need to do is call a time-out and talk to an adult.

What if criminal actions are disclosed during the mediation?

If any illegal activity or threats of illegal activity are disclosed during the mediation process, mediators should disclose that to an adult.

STEP FIVE
Follow-Up to Training

■ *BUILDING CONFIDENCE*

Once the training has been completed and the program has begun, there are many considerations for ongoing improvement. It is very important that mediators be given positive reinforcement frequently. Newly trained mediators are anxious to use their skills but are very nervous about making mistakes. Stress to them that making mistakes is to be expected and in fact will make them stronger mediators as they learn from those mistakes.

Also, mediators must be prepared for difficulties while mediating. Not all mediations go as smoothly as the role plays did in the training sessions. Encourage students to use common sense and rely on each other and their trained teachers for guidance and support. If it is necessary for mediators to call a time-out for an unforeseen problem occurring during the mediation, encourage them to do so. They have the option of conferring with an adult and continuing the mediation or postponing the mediation until they have time to discuss the problem with an adult. The comfort of the mediators is a priority!

■ *EVALUATING THE PROGRAM*

By keeping a record of the date and number of mediations done each year, the grade and gender of the disputants, the individuals making the referrals, and whether or not mediations ended with a written agreement, the success of the mediation program can be evaluated (see Exhibit 7.1, a sample tracking form). Having such data available is also an excellent way to inform administrators, faculty and staff, students, and parents about how the program was used throughout the school year. A heavily used program is not indicative of a school in crisis but, rather, an indication that the program was recognized as a successful way of handling conflict. In fact, the more mediations that are done, the less likely it is that small episodes of conflict will escalate into something more serious.

■ *PLANNING FOR ONGOING TRAINING*

Meeting with mediators on a regular basis to give them time to practice their mediation skills is most beneficial. It also gives them a chance to discuss unique problems and situations that have arisen during mediations. By sharing ideas and experiences, mediators will strengthen their skills. Such meetings are sometimes difficult due to time constraints. If that is the case, a day can be taken to run a refresher class for trained mediators early in the school year.

Older, more experienced mediators can be a tremendous resource in helping to develop the skills of younger, less experienced ones. Consider inviting a high school mediation team to lunch or a rap session with intermediate mediators to discuss experiences. Elementary mediators can gain valuable knowledge from intermediate students. Educational Mediation Services of Lancaster, Pennsylvania, sponsors a mediation summit with the governor of Pennsylvania each spring, where thousands of mediators from across the state convene at the state capitol to share experiences and ideas with other mediation teams.

■ *HAVE FUN!*

Mediation is a process that must be taken seriously, but it is also important that mediators be given opportunities to have fun and to sponsor activities within the school to foster camaraderie and school spirit. A school dance with an antiviolence theme is one suggestion. This is also a good way to raise money for special activities, such as a summit, end-of-the-year picnic, or luncheon following the training.

Last, it's a good idea to bring closure to the school year and celebrate the success of the program by providing the mediators and their trained faculty members with something enjoyable and relaxing. This might be a field trip, an outing, or a picnic. Sharing this experience with other teams within the district or with a neighboring district's mediation teams can also be most enjoyable.

Exhibit 7.1. Tracking Form

Names	Date	Gender	Grade	Referral Source	Agreement Y/N
1. a. Jane Doe	4-1-99	F	8th	Mr. Will	Y
b. Mary Reed	4-1-99	F	7th		
2. a.					
b.					
3. a.					
b.					
4. a.					
b.					
5. a.					
b.					
6. a.					
b.					
7. a.					
b.					
8. a.					
b.					
9. a.					
b.					
10. a.					
b.					

■ *EXPANDING THE PROGRAM*

Once the program has been established and accepted in the school, there are innumerable possibilities for expanding the process. Possibilities include the following:

- Mediations between parents and children
- Mediations between parents
- Mediations between siblings
- Mediations between faculty members
- Mediations between teachers and students

■ *PROGRAM EVALUATION*

To monitor and continue to improve the effectiveness of a peer mediation program, an evaluation process needs to be established. As with any new program, positive change takes place over time. It would be detrimental to any new program to expect immediate, noticeable changes. As more and more students use the program, word of the program's success will spread, resulting in both positive change and heavier use of the program itself. Another important consideration in evaluating the program is that a peer mediation program will *not* necessarily decrease the number of physical fights in and around the school. Although it can, to use this as a measurement of success would be detrimental. One needs to ask if there would have been more fights had the program not been in existence. More important factors are the number of signed agreements and recidivism rates (continuing conflicts between particular pairs of students). Recidivism is rare and can be tracked via the tracking form (Exhibit 7.1).

Because the objectives of a peer mediation program are to improve school climate and reduce violence in and around the school, an effective tool for evaluation is a survey and observation form to be filled out by students, faculty, staff, and administration (see Exhibit 7.2). The results gathered from this survey, along with comparative data from the administration on student behavior, suspensions, and expulsions, provide a comprehensive look at the effectiveness of the program.

Exhibit 7.2. Peer Mediation Survey and Observation Form

Please circle the most appropriate answer

1. I am a(n)
   a. teacher   b. student   c. administrator   d. staff member   e. mediator

2. I have used the peer mediation process.
   a. yes   b. no

3. I am satisfied with my experience in peer mediation.
   a. yes   b. no   c. I have not used it.

4. I have used peer mediation more than once.
   a. yes (how many times? _____)   b. no   c. I have not used it at all.

5. If you have not used peer mediation, what has been the reason?
   a. I have not had the need.   b. I did not know what it   c. I did not know how to   d. I don't trust it.
                                           was about.   be referred.

6. If I had a conflict, I would consider using peer mediation.
   a. yes   b. no   c. I'm not sure.

7. I have referred students to the peer mediation process.
   a. yes   b. no

8. I have encouraged people to use peer mediation.
   a. yes   b. no

9. I think peer mediation has made a positive difference at our school.
   a. yes   b. no

Gilhooley, J., & Scheuch, N. *Using Peer Mediation in Classrooms and Schools: Strategies for Teachers, Counselors, and Administrators.* © 2000 Corwin Press, Inc.

■ *CONCLUSION*

Although violence in our society cannot be blamed on the schools, our schools are microcosms of society. Therefore, we believe that the schools are a logical place to begin solving this problem. For change to be made on a large scale, we need to begin with our children. We feel strongly that we can teach students the skills to resolve conflicts peacefully through mutual respect and understanding of feelings, active listening, and cooperative problem solving. Peer mediation programs, over the course of time, can lead to the development of citizens as self-regulating members of society. This is turn will lead to more peaceful and productive schools and a less violent society as well.

Resource:
Sample Training Posters

Training Poster 1 _____

Training Agenda

Day 1

Ground rules

Understanding conflict

Conflict resolution styles

Finding solutions

Feelings

Active listening

Paraphrasing

Day 2

Points of view

Introduction stage

Managing anger

Storytelling stage

Brainstorming

Problem solving

Day 3

Agreement writing

Confidentiality

Full-mediation roll-play

Evaluation

Certificates

Training Poster 2 _____

Ground Rules

- Everyone should participate.

- Respect the feelings and ideas of others.

- Be supportive of others.

- Respect confidentiality.

- *Have fun!!!*

Gilhooley, J., & Scheuch, N. *Using Peer Mediation in Classrooms and Schools: Strategies for Teachers, Counselors, and Administrators.* © 2000 Corwin Press, Inc.

Training Poster 3 _____

Conflict

Training Poster 4 _____

Conflict Resolution Styles

-

-

-

Does the problem get solved?

What happens to the relationship?

Training Poster 5 _____

Finding Solutions

Lose/Lose

Win/Lose

Win/Win

Training Poster 6 _____

Why Mediation Works

Mediation

- Is based on respect

- Is voluntary

- Stresses cooperation

- Allows exploring options

- Encourages expression of emotions

- Examines the other's point of view

- Results in a win/win outcome

Training Poster 7 _____

Feelings of Conflict

Training Poster 8 _____

Thoughts
Versus Feelings

"I feel like . . ." expresses a thought.

"I feel . . ." expresses a feeling.

Which are the following?

"I feel like punching him."

"I feel frustrated."

"I feel hurt."

"I feel like no one cares."

"I feel like he should apologize."

Training Poster 9 _____

Active Listening

1.

2.

3.

4.

5.

6.

What kind of listener are you?

Training Poster 10 _____

Paraphrasing

Paraphrasing is summarizing a story for *facts and feelings:*

"So, what you're saying is . . ."

"And you're feeling . . ."

"Is that correct?"

Gilhooley, J., & Scheuch, N. *Using Peer Mediation in Classrooms and Schools: Strategies for Teachers, Counselors, and Administrators.* © 2000 Corwin Press, Inc.

Training Poster 11 _____

Mediation Process

1. Introduction

2. Storytelling

3. Problem Solving

4. Agreement

Training Poster 12 _____

Introduction Stage

Be Confident

1. Make introductions.

2. Review the ground rules:

   Do you agree to no interruptions?

   Do you agree to no name calling?

   Do you agree to tell the truth?

   Do you agree to work hard to solve the problem?

Training Poster 13 _____

Things That Make Me Angry

Training Poster 14 _____

Things I Do or Say
When I'm Angry

Training Poster 15 _____

"I" Messages

"I" messages are nonthreatening ways to express anger without putting others on the defensive.

"I feel . . .

when you . . .

because . . ."

Training Poster 16 _____

Storytelling Stage

First, mediators say:

1. "Tell us what happened." "How did you feel?"

   Mediators paraphrase for *facts and feelings.*

Next, mediators say:

2. "Tell us what you heard _____ say."

   "How is he or she feeling?"

   "Is that correct?"

Have the disputants paraphrase for *facts and feelings.*

Training Poster 17 _____

Brainstorming

1. Decide what you want to serve at your party.

2. You and your partner make a list of ten items.

3. Cross out what you don't agree on.

4. What remains is your party list.

5. Are you happy with your choices?

Gilhooley, J., & Scheuch, N. *Using Peer Mediation in Classrooms and Schools: Strategies for Teachers, Counselors, and Administrators.* © 2000 Corwin Press, Inc.

Training Poster 18 _____

Problem Solving

1. "What can you do to solve this problem?"

   Mediators list disputants' options on the agreement form.

2. "Can you agree to this?"

   Mediators go over the list of options crossing out those that the disputants don't agree on.

3. "When can you do this?"

   Mediators ask *when* disputants will do what they have agree on.

Training Poster 19 _____

Agreement Stage

1. Mediators restate those solutions agreed to by both disputants.

2. Mediators ask,

   "Is the problem solved for both of you?"

3. Mediators ask,

   "What can keep this from happening again?"

4. Everyone signs the agreement.

   "Congratulations! You solved your problem."

   > Congratulate yourselves!!!
   > You did it!!!

Training Poster 20 _____

You Did It!

Congratulations

You Did It!

Peer Mediation

has successfully completed peer mediation training.

Date: _____

Trainer: _____

Index

**CORWIN
PRESS**

The Corwin Press logo—a raven striding across an open book—represents the happy union of courage and learning. We are a professional-level publisher of books and journals for K-12 educators, and we are committed to creating and providing resources that embody these qualities. Corwin's motto is "Success for All Learners."

FEB 0 . 2009